Family Walks
on the Isle of Anglesey

Laurence Main

HIGH INTEREST · LOW MILEAGE

Scarthin Books of Cromford
Derbyshire
1993

Family Walks Series

General Editor: Norman Taylor

The Country Code

Guard against all risk of fire
Fasten all gates
Keep your dogs under proper control
Keep to public paths across farmland
Avoid damaging fences, hedges and walls
Leave no litter
Safeguard water supplies
Make no unnecessary noise
Protect wildlife, plants and trees
Go carefully along country roads
Respect the life of the countryside

Walking the routes in this book

All the routes in this book have been walked, in most cases, several times prior to publication and we have taken great care to ensure that they are on rights of way. However, changes occur all the time in the landscape; should you meet any obstructions, please let us know. Serious obstructions can be brought to the attention of the local branch of the Ramblers Association and the Rights of Way section of the County Council.

Published 1993

Phototypesetting, printing by The Alden Press, Oxford

ISBN 0 907758 665

Cover illustration by Andrew Ravenwood

The Dingle, Llangefni (route 9)

Preface

Islands are places apart, equipped to enchant. Anglesey is such a place, full of ancient stones, hermits' cells and spellbinding coves and beaches. There is also a perfect moated castle and the railway station with the longest name in British Rail. Yet it is so easy to cross one of the two bridges over the Menai Strait and fail to realise where you are. Many keep driving all the way to the Irish ferry in Holyhead and only know Anglesey from the A5. Travel has become too easy and unfulfilling. Spend time exploring the ancient public footpaths, however, and you will have no doubt where you are. You will have been in touch with the land and absorbed some of its secrets. Anglesey is just the right size to get to know in the family summer holiday. There is a good public transport network to help you get around and there are plenty of places to visit. Couple this with the exotic feeling of being where Welsh is spoken and you have the ingredients for a memorable family walking holiday.

Acknowledgements

As usual, these walks were reached by public transport and many kindnesses and courtesies were experienced. Bus drivers, ticket office clerks and fellow passengers can be delightful bonuses to journeys. Our visit was made in January, so we proved that Anglesey is a good place for a walking holiday at any time in the year. We have been to the island several times and camped in August, which was very enjoyable. This time we stayed in bed and breakfast accommodation and can report that it was excellent. We found the address in *The Ramblers' Yearbook and Accommodation Guide* (free to members of the Ramblers' Association). Well done, Mrs Simms!

About the Author

Laurence Main is the author of over 30 footpath guidebooks, including four other titles in the Family Walks series, covering Mid Wales, Snowdonia, Oxfordshire and the Isle of Wight. He is a full-time writer and contributes regularly to walking magazines, including *Country Walking* and *Trail Walker*, plus the *Western Mail*. Married with four children (two boys and two girls), Laurence is the voluntary footpaths secretary for the Ramblers' Association in Meirionnydd, where he has lived since 1981.

Contents

Location Map of the Walks

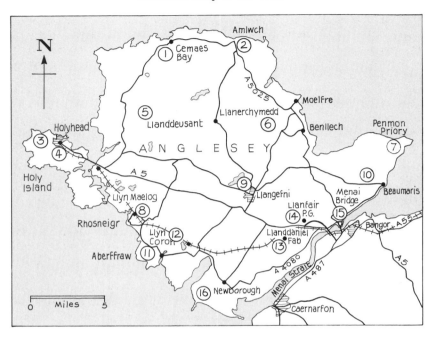

The view of Newborough Forest from Ynys Llanddwyn (route 16)

Introduction

This is a book of short, undemanding walks that you could take your granny or your toddler on. Only one of the walks reaches four miles in length but each has its own special feature to attract and stimulate young minds. This could be a castle or a lake famous for its birdlife. The sea is never far away on this island, so there are beaches, clifftop paths and shipwrecks. There are also Neolithic burial chambers, Roman forts, an excitingly long harbour breakwater, a windmill and a water mill, viewpoints, a column you can climb, a suspension bridge you can go under, holy wells, tales of saints and even older legends, a wooded dingle, the site of the old royal palace and a modern exhibition to teach you about it. Much of Anglesey is a plateau but you won't find anywhere dull. Indeed everywhere seems to be brought within reach. A short climb gives the impression of having gained the summit of a mountain.

Anglesey is a detached part of Snowdonia's coastal plain. It was made into an island during the Ice Age. Glaciers flowing south from the Irish Sea combined with those flowing down from the mountains. When they melted, a valley or series of valleys was left to become the Menai Strait. Similarly, Holy Island was cut off from the rest of Anglesey. The channels weren't wide, but considerable enough when there is also a vicious current. The island is fairly compact, covering some 280 square miles and measuring about 23 miles across at its widest points. Some of the rocks are really ancient, being pre-Cambrian or over 600 millions years old. Limestone and shale were deposited on top of these, while the melting of the glaciers left a topsoil of boulder clay. This blessed the island with highly fertile soil and probably accounts for the evidence of a relatively high population in prehistoric times. The current population is about 70,000, of whom about 60% are Welsh-speakers.

There were far more trees, especially oak and hazel, when the first settlers arrived. Neolithic people were clearing the dense forests by 2500 BC. They have left a large number of monuments to ponder over. Bryn Celli Ddu is one of the best preserved chamber tombs in Britain. It is too old for us to know about the religion of the people who constructed it but we do know about the druids, and Anglesey was their sanctuary. The Romans moved to take it and then fortified the island against the Irish. Contact with Ireland was not new, as the traditional tale of Branwen reveals (see Route 11). She spent her wedding night on Anglesey and was buried here. When Roman power waned, however, the Britons had to call for help from the mighty Cunedda. He founded the dynasty which made Gwynedd the great power in Wales and Anglesey was Gwynedd's granary. The island's ancient Welsh name is Mon (the Romans called it Mona) and is known as 'Mon Mam Cymru' (Anglesey, the mother of Wales). Her fat, fertile, plains provide the nation with its food. The climate is mild, with less rain and more sunshine than Snowdonia. Snow is rare and lambs are born early in the winter. Indian summers, known in Welsh as 'haf bach codi tatws' (a little summer for lifting potatoes) are common.

Make a practice of carrying the relevant Ordnance Survey Pathfinder map (at a scale of $2\frac{1}{2}''$ to one mile) on your walks. The relevant numbers are given on each route map, which is drawn at an even more generous scale to show stiles, gates and other features. Older children can be taught to use a compass. Then, instead of looking across the Menai Strait at Snowdonia, they'll soon be exploring the mountains for themselves, having gained the necessary experience in the relative safety of Anglesey.

Some of the most delightful moments are when you meet a friendly farmer. This is when your knowledge of, or just willingness to learn, Welsh will stand you in good stead. Please don't bring dogs onto sheep pasture.

The Welsh Language

Welsh is a living language spoken by half a million people just a few miles away from English cities such as Liverpool and Birmingham. The Welsh language and the cultural heritage that goes with it is ignored on the eastern side of Offa's Dyke, however. English schoolchildren know more about the Greeks and Romans than they do about the heroes and heroines of *The Mabinogion*, the great collection of ancient Welsh literature. Now the schools are the main hope for the future of Welsh. More and more English migrants are putting at risk the dominance of the old tongue. Their children can be taught to become fluent Welsh-speakers, however. There are plenty of books to help the beginner to learn. Even you could acquire a few words and phrases. Try these:

Good morning – Bore da (Bor-eh-da)
Good afternoon – Prnhawn da (Pre-noun-da)
Good evening – Noswaith da (Noss-wa-eeth-da)
Please – Os gwelwch yn dda (Oss-gwe-loo-kin-tha)
Thank you very much – Diolch yn fawr (Dee-olc-hen-vawr)
It's fine today – Mae hi'n braf heddiw (My-heen-brav-heth-you)

Melin Llynon (Llynon Windmill), Llanddeusant, route 5

Symbols used on the route maps

Symbol	Description	Symbol	Description
↑	The footpath route with direction from the start	③	Number corresponding with route directions
⋯⋅⋅	Other paths (not always rights of way)	▰	Railway
⫽	Motor road	⤳	River or stream with direction of flow
⤙⤚⤙⤚	Hedge or fence	⤳⤝⤳	Bridge
∘∘∘∘∘	Wall	ϙϙϙ	Trees
o	Standing stone, column or tower	▪▪	Buildings
G	Gate	▫	Ruin
S	Stile	+	Church or chapel
P	Signpost	⊓	Castle
T	Telephone box	⋈	Chambered cairn
PO	Post Office	⋇	Windmill
BUS	Bus stop		
⇌	Railway station	↑ N	Direction of North (not always at the top of the map)
OS	Relevant ordnance survey pathfinder map		

(The whole island is covered by the Ordnance Survey Landranger map no 114 – Anglesey)

Each map has a scale in miles and a gradient profile showing the height in feet above sea level and the distance in miles from the start.

9

The coast path north of Amlwch, overlooking East Mouse (Ynys Amlwch) (Route 2)

Cemaes Bay

Outline
Cemaes – Traeth Mawr – National Trust Clifftop Path – Llanbadrig – Glan-yr-afon – Traeth Mawr – Cemaes.

Summary
Children must be well supervised on the clifftop path, but it is well-maintained by the National Trust and allows impressive views. Visit a church commemorating the fact that St Patrick visited this spot and return along a lane past the childhood home of an interesting seaman. The sandy beach awaits you as you approach Cemaes.

Attractions
The little harbour village of Cemaes could belong to Cornwall. It has an inviting sandy beach and lies between Wylfa nuclear power station and the National Trust's headlands on the eastern side of the bay. This was the chief port on Anglesey's north coast until the Industrial Revolution caused the growth of Amlwch. Smuggling used to be endemic, while fishing boats were based at the port which had its own thriving shipbuilding industry.

Many of the locals now work for Wylfa, where the nuclear power station was opened in 1971. It is a Magnox reactor and could soon be closed, thus making hundreds of local people redundant. The sinister shape of its buildings on the skyline is a powerful incentive to accept the presence of windmills, however. It is built on the coastline because 55 million gallons of sea water are needed every hour for cooling purposes.

The clifftop path that begins from the car-park at the eastern end of Traeth Mawr (the beach) is a colourful corridor for naturalists. The purple of knapweed combines with the blue of sheep's bit, the white of wild carrot and the yellow cat's ear, while painted ladies and red admirals flutter by. Descend to the northern beach, where a solitary white rock gives it the English name of White Lady Bay.

St Patrick is said to have been saved from shipwreck here in the fifth century and the nearby church is the only one in Wales dedicated to him. The medieval church building was restored in the 19th century by Lord Stanley of Alderley. This uncle of the philosopher Bertrand Russell was a Moslem and there is an Islamic influence to the stained glass windows. The church had to be restored after vandals burned it down in 1985. Rock pipits perch on the gravestones in the ancient churchyard before they swoop on flies.

The lane back to Cemaes passes Glan-yr-afon. This was the childhood home of William Owen, who became one of Anglesey's most famous seamen. William was actually born, in 1837, on the other side of Cemaes, at a small holding known as Tan Y Fron. Like most dwellings at that time it had insanitary floors of bare earth, damp

Continued on page 14

11

Route 1

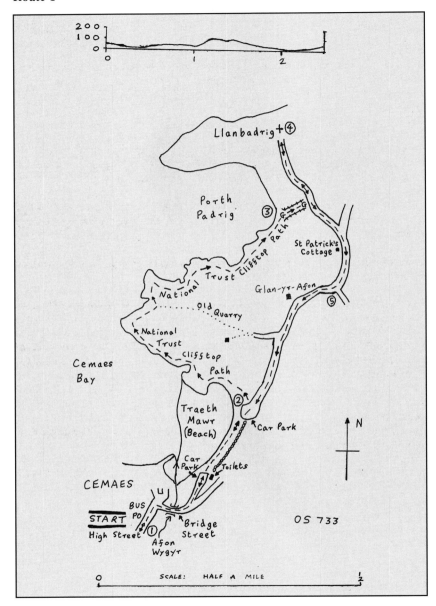

Route 1

Cemaes Bay

$2\frac{1}{2}$ **miles**

Start

Cemaes is four miles west of Amlwch on the A5025. The bus stop in Cemaes High Street is near the Post Office (GR SH 374934). There are car-parks at both ends of the beach (Traeth Mawr).

Route

1. *Face the Post Office and go right along Cemaes High Street. Turn right down Bridge Street to cross the Afon Wygyr. Fork left down to the beach, passing a car-park and public toilets. Continue past the beach on your left.*

2. *Turn left along the National Trust Clifftop Path. Follow it with great care, keeping above Cemaes Bay on your left. Reach the beach at Porth Padrig (White Lady Bay).*

3. *Bear right, inland, through a kissing-gate and along an enclosed path to a lane. Go left to the church at Llanbadrig.*

4. *Retrace your steps along the lane and go right at a junction to pass St Patrick's Cottage on your right.*

5. *Fork right along the lane to pass Glan-yr-afon on your right. Return to the beach (Traeth Mawr) and pass it on your right this time as you retrace your steps into Cemaes.*

Public Transport

Bus no. 61 runs on weekdays from Bangor to Cemaes via Amlwch. Bus no. 62 from Holyhead to Cemaes continues to Amlwch.

walls and a leaking roof. Sanitation consisted of a bucket which was emptied, when full, in a nearby stream. Drinking water came from the village well, while at night the family slept 4 to a bed. William was soon sent to live with his aunt at Glan-yr-afon, where he wasn't happy. He ran away to sea at the age of 8 and by 1858 was the mate or master of a small ship which sailed around the coast and as far as the Mediterranean and the Baltic. William Owen's career is then recorded at the Liverpool Maritime Museum. He became a pilot, moved back from Liverpool to Anglesey with a wife and four children and, as a special pilot with the White Star Line, had the honour of piloting the royal yacht into Liverpool with King Edward VII on board in 1904. Awarded the Royal Victorian Order for services to his sovereign, he retired as a pilot in 1906 and from an advisory role in 1911. He died on Anglesey in 1914.

Refreshments
Cemaes has shops and the Stag Inn, near the harbour.

The Gorsedd Stone Circle, Menai Bridge (Route 15)

14

Amlwch

Outline
Amlwch – Traeth Dynion – Coast Path – Pwll y Merched – Amlwch.

Summary
Follow paths past gorse bushes between Amlwch and the sea, then follow a rugged section of Anglesey's Coast Path before returning inland along a walled track.

Attractions
Amlwch boasted the world's largest copper port around 1800. It served the copper mines on Parys Mountain, just to the south. Despite the association with industry, the jagged rocks of this coastline assert the triumph of nature. They also wrecked a transatlantic liner in 1877. The Romans had mined Parys Mountain for copper but the metal's importance soared with the invention of cannons in the late Middle Ages. Up to 44,000 tons of ore a year were produced in the late 18th and early 19th centuries. The fishing hamlet that was Amlwch was transformed into a town of 6000 people and over 1000 alehouses. The Parys Mines Company built St Eilian's church in 1800. They destroyed Parys Mountain, however, with the whole of the 489 ft high hill being mined away.

There is still a chemical works here and its freight traffic has kept the railway line open. This runs for 19 miles from the mainline at Gaerwen and opened as the Anglesey Central Railway in 1866. Passenger services (via Llangefni) ceased in 1964 but while the freight traffic remains there is hope of their being revived.

The transatlantic liner wrecked by the rocks was the *Dakota*. This steamer was built at Newcastle in 1874 as a challenger for the Blue Riband. When she was wrecked on 9 May 1877 she was on her way from Liverpool to New York. Weighing 4332 tons and steaming at 14 knots 2 miles offshore, she was steered inland and wrecked on rocks between the chemical works and the offshore island known as East Mouse or Ynys Amlwch. The Bull Bay lifeboat made a series of trips to rescue her 218 passengers, then the mail being carried to America and as much as possible of her 2000 tons of general cargo. The liner's 401 ft long iron hull is popular with divers.

Refreshments
There is a choice in Amlwch.

Route 2

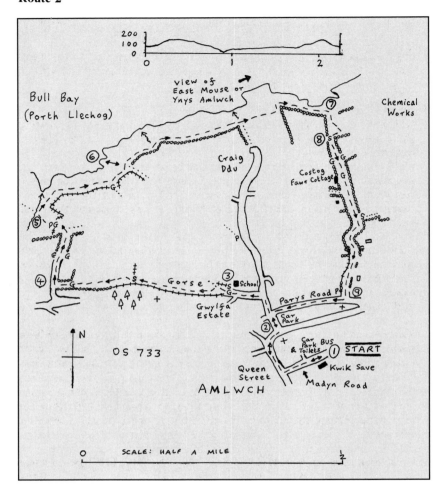

Route 2

Amlwch

2¼ miles

Start

> *Buses stop in Madyn Road outside Kwik Save. There is a car-park here, but if you're not shopping at Kwik Save there is another at direction no. 2, between Stryd Mona and Lon Parys (GR SH 444929).*

Route

1. *Go down Madyn Road to Queen Street (Stryd y Frenhines) and turn right, passing the Queen's Head on the corner. Go past St Eilian's church on your right and turn right along Stryd Mona.*

2. *In a short distance turn left to pass the public library on your left and a car-park on your right. Go ahead across Lon Parys (Parys Road) and turn left along an access road passing a school on your right. Do not bear left with this down into the Gwylfa estate.*

3. *Go ahead across a stile next to a gate. Bear left with the path to walk past gorse bushes. Continue with a fence on your left and pass the distinctive shape of Amlwch's Roman Catholic chapel. This is meant to represent an upturned boat. Go ahead over a stile, pass a plantation of trees on your left and go forward along a walled path to its junction with a lane.*

4. *Turn right along the lane, which deteriorates as it approaches the sea and ends in a space used for parking cars. Bear left with the signposted Coast Path, going through a kissing-gate and descending to a creek. Do not cross the stream!*

5. *Turn right to walk with the stream on your left towards the sea. Bear right with a fence on your right to walk along the clifftops with the sea on your left. Do not be tempted by a kissing-gate on your right but do venture down steps to the beach on your left.*

6. *Climb back up the steps to resume walking along the Coast Path with the sea on your left. When the wall on your right ends, go ahead to another wall and go left to follow it around on your right. East Mouse, the offshore island known in Welsh as Ynys Amlwch, can be seen ahead.*

7. *When this wall turns inland, go right too but veer slightly left to a wall ahead. Turn right to walk with this wall on your left to a stile in the corner.*

8. *Go left along a walled track which passes Costog Fawr Cottage on your right. Continue, ignoring another track forking right, to reach Lon Parys.*

Continued on page 18

17

9. *Turn right along Lon Parys to rejoin your outward route near the public library and retrace your steps to the bus stop near Kwik Save.*

Public Transport

There is a daily bus service (no. 63) from Bangor, plus a more frequent weekday service from Bangor and Cemaes (no. 62). The no. 61 bus links Amlwch with Holyhead on weekdays, the no. 231 runs from Moelfre on Mondays, Wednesdays and Fridays only and the no. 232 runs from Llangefni on Thursdays only, while the no. 32 provides a more frequent weekday service from Llangefni.

This part of the old tramway is now signposted as a section of the Coastal Footpath (Route 3)

Soldier's Point

Outline

Holyhead Sailing Club (Link with Route 4) – Soldier's Point – Clifftop Path – Dismantled Tramway – Soldier's Point – Holyhead Sailing Club (Link with Route 4).

Summary

A quiet access lane leads to the start of the breakwater whose construction was responsible for the quarries and tramway. Before exploring this little bit of industrial archaeology, however, enjoy the magnificence of nature in what will probably be a raw wind but on a fine path where the cliffs are relatively safe.

Attractions

Holyhead's breakwater is an extremely impressive structure. The longest in Britain, it makes a fine promenade of one and a half miles (with obvious consideration for children's safety). It stands 39 feet above the low water mark. Its origin can be dated back to the decision of Parliament in 1828 to build harbours of refuge all around Britain so that passing ships could ride out gales. Work started in 1845 under the direction of the civil engineer James Meadows Rendal. He died in 1856 and the work was completed by John Hawkshaw, who built himself the square, white, castellated house on Soldier's Point. Limestone was quarried on Holyhead Mountain and carried along a tramway. It was dumped in the sea at the rate of 24,000 tons a week and the Prince of Wales opened the breakwater in 1873. The New Harbour thus created could shelter at least 100 ships in the event of a storm.

If you require a really strenuous route up rocky paths to the 722 ft summit of Holyhead Mountain (the highest point on the island), follow the OS Pathfinder map with care and note that these tortuous ways are not for beginners. Your reward on a clear day could be a view of Ireland's Wicklow Mountains. The quarries are now a country park, after continuing to produce limestone which was pulverized into house bricks and exported from Holyhead.

Yes, Soldier's Point is meant to be in the singular! An Admiralty store room and a defensive battery were situated here. If you do venture, with caution, along the breakwater, you'll come to where the *Kirkmichael*, a rigged barque of 933 tons, sank on 22 December 1894. A storm caused her to sail for the shelter of the harbour but she failed to round the breakwater and lies near the outer side about 300 yards from the old lighthouse, between a large repair to the wall and outlet pipes. Two of her crew of 14 died, despite the brave rescuers crawling along the breakwater, dragging their gear towards them in the teeth of a gale and high sea.

Refreshments

Plenty of choice in Holyhead (Route 4).

Route 3

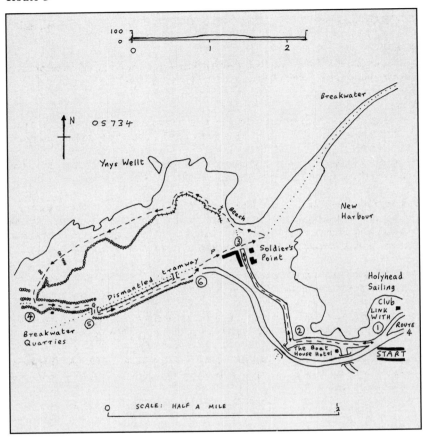

Route 3

Soldier's Point

$2\frac{1}{4}$ **miles**

Start

This walk is best linked with Route 4 (Holyhead Roman Fort) at the road junction near Holyhead Sailing Club (GR SH 241833).

Route

1. With your back to the sea, bear right along the road which keeps closer to the shore. With the New Harbour on your right, pass the Boat House Hotel on your left.

2. Follow the road as it bends right, ignoring a path under the road on your left. Eventually reach the end of the road at Soldier's Point.

3. Turn right along the course of the dismantled tramway towards the breakwater. Turn sharply left before it, however, to descend to a beach. Bear left over a stile and follow a fence on your left, keeping the sea on your right. Go ahead along a well-trodden path which becomes surfaced and bears left between walls.

4. Turn left along a walled track. Take a kissing-gate to cross a wooden bridge over the course of the dismantled tramway.

5. Turn left to walk with a fence on your left and a wall on your right. Pass a second bridge on your left, go ahead and fork left down to the old tramway.

6. Go right along the course of the old tramway, towards the breakwater. When you reach the end of your access road on your right, turn right to walk back along it towards Holyhead.

Public Transport

Link this walk with Route 4 and start at the bus stop near the railway station in Holyhead.

A yacht at Holyhead Sailing Club

Holyhead Roman Fort

Outline

Holyhead Station – Roman Fort – Newry Street – Holyhead Sailing Club
(Link with Route 3) – Tourist Information Centre – Holyhead Station.

Summary

Now that you can step off a train straight onto the Irish ferry, many travellers fail to
explore this fine old port. For students of Roman history it offers a fine coastal fort,
while bird-watchers congregate to overlook the New Harbour.

Attractions

It's usual to see names in both Welsh and English in Wales, but the guesthouses of
Holyhead know to translate theirs into Gaelic too. The Irish tourists who respond
to this will find Holyhead an interesting place. The largest town in Anglesey, it has
offered a ferry service to Ireland for centuries. While you're here, why not take a day
trip to Dublin?

Historically, the Welsh were more interested in keeping the Irish invaders out of
their country. Solid evidence of this is provided by the actual Roman walls on the
north, west and south sides of the Roman coastal fort now in the centre of the town.
These walls are extremely well preserved. Their internal height is about 13 ft and
they are 5 feet thick. The fort has a sub-rectangular shape, about 246 ft by 148 ft.
There were originally four corner towers, although the south-west one is largely
destroyed.

Caer Gybi (Cybi's Castle) is the Welsh name for Holyhead. Cybi was a 6th
century saint who was granted this site for a monastic foundation by Maelgwn
Gwynedd. The 13th century church standing within the walls may mark the site of
this foundation. Naturally, the church is dedicated to St Cybi. A small chapel in the
fort's south-western corner is known as Eglwys y Bedd (Church of the Grave). It
may cover St Cybi's grave. An alternative view is that the grave is that of Seregri,
leader of a band of Irish invaders. Maelgwn Gwynedd was a descendant of
Cunedda who came down from the region just north of Hadrian's wall after the
withdrawal of the Roman legions in 410 AD and expelled the Irish before
establishing a powerful dynasty. Whoever lies under it, the chapel is known to have
been built in the 14th century and became a schoolhouse for the poor children of the
parish in 1748.

Winter is when bird-watchers come to Holyhead to view the birds in the New
Harbour. These include red-throated diver, black-throated diver, great northern
diver, little grebe, red-necked grebe, black guillemot, pochard, common scoter, red-
breasted merganser, shearwaters, petrels, gannet, auks, gulls, terns and sea duck.

Route 4

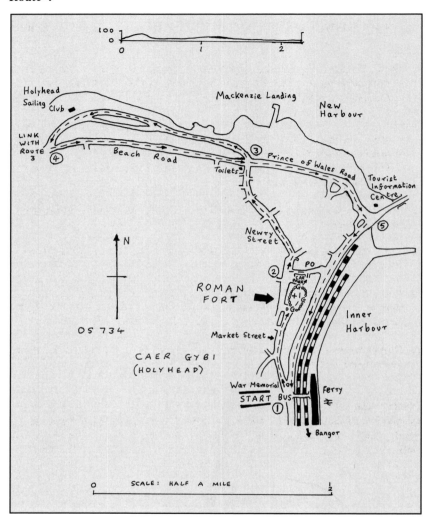

Route 4

Holyhead Roman Fort $2\frac{1}{4}$ miles

Start

The walk begins from the bus stop outside Holyhead's railway station (also the nearest public transport for Route 3, which links with this one). There is a car-park just to the north of the Roman fort (GR SH 247823).

Route

1. With your back to the railway, cross the road to the war memorial and bear right up to Market Street. Take the gate into the Roman fort at its end and walk past St Cybi's church on your left. Go ahead through the gate cut into the Roman wall to reach a car-park. Go left to Stanley Street.

2. Turn right and soon fork left to follow Newry Street towards the sea. Cross Prince of Wales Road.

3. Bear left down the road which follows the shore to Holyhead Sailing Club. Bear left inland to Beach Road (and the link with Route 3).

4. Turn left along the pavement of Beach Road to walk with a fine view over the New Harbour on your left. Continue along Prince of Wales Road to Marine Square. The Tourist Information Centre is on your left.

5. Turn right along Victoria Road to walk with the railway on your left back to the bus stop beside the station.

Public Transport

Ferries from Ireland, trains from England and buses from Bangor (including a Sunday service, no. 44) and various parts of the island converge on the start of this walk.

The north-eastern tower of Holyhead's Roman Fort

Turn right immediately after this pump in Llanddeusant

Llanddeusant

Outline
Llanddeusant – Melin Hywel – Melin Llynon – Llanddeusant.

Summary
Anglesey has plenty of wind and water. This walk takes you to see both put to good use – at a water mill and a windmill. Fieldpaths, which may be damp in places, lead to a firm track and roads.

Attractions
The first mill you come to on this walk is Melin Hywel and it is powered by water. It still produces animal feed and visitors are usually welcome during the summer. There was a mill here in 1335, while the present building was enlarged in 1850 and restored in 1975. It is privately owned.

Anglesey Borough Council deserve congratulations for buying, restoring and re-opening a windmill, Melin Llynon. They used to be common on the island but this is now the only working windmill in Wales. Llynon is a typical Anglesey mill, with its stone tower tapering towards the top. There are three storeys inside and the three sets of millstones are on the first floor. The tower supports the windshaft, sails and wooden cap, all of which has to be turned manually to head the sails into the wind. The mill was built in 1775 and 1776 and the first miller, Thomas Jones, must have started young because he died in 1846 at the age of 90. After his son and grandsons, Robert Rowlands acquired the tenancy in 1893 and saw the mill decline. Storm damage in 1918 locked the cap in one position and allowed milling to continue only when the wind was in the right quarter. The cost of repairing it couldn't be justified as the railways distributed cheap factory-milled flour. The mill was left to decay in 1923 and each winter took its toll until a storm in 1954 removed most of the cap and allowed the rain to enter freely. The Council moved to purchase the mill and restore it but this didn't happen until 1978. By then it was virtually impossible to buy the necessary 'bent' timbers for the boat-shaped cap and the long beams of matured pitch pine for the sail whips. The job was done by 1984, however, with an outbuilding converted into a cafe and information point. Transport yourself back 200 years as the sails turn to produce stoneground wholemeal flour. The mill is open during the summer from Tuesdays to Saturdays between 11 am and 5 pm, plus Sundays from 1 pm to 5 pm. Telephone 0407 730797 for further information (0407 840845 in winter).

Bedd Branwen, nearby at grid reference SH 361850, is the traditional burial place of Branwen, heroine of one of the stories in *The Mabinogion*.

Refreshments
There is a cafe at Melin Llynon.

27

Route 5

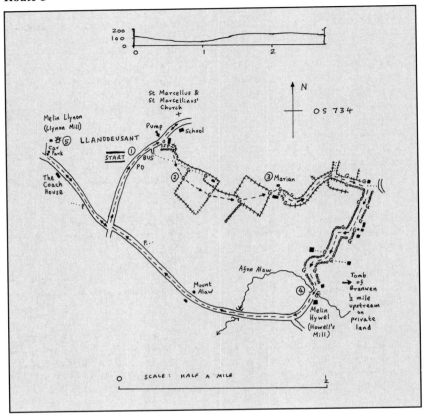

200
100
0
0   1   2

Melin Llynon
(Llynon Mill)

Car Park

(5) LLANDDEUSANT

START (1)

St Marcellus &
St Marcellinus'
Church
+

Pump

School

BUS
PO

N

OS 734

The
Coach
House

P

(2) G   G

G   G

(3) Marian

G   G
G

G   G   G

G
G

P

Afon Alaw

Mount
Alaw

G
G

G
G

(4)

Melin
Hywel
(Howell's
Mill)

G
G   G

Tomb
of
Branwen
½ mile
upstream
on
private
land

0   SCALE :   HALF A MILE   ½

28

Route 5

Llanddeusant

$2\frac{3}{4}$ miles

Start

Llanddeusant lies two miles east of the A5025 about 12 miles south-west of Amlwch. This walk is described from the bus stop near the Post Office in Llanddeusant (GR SH 345852).

Route

1. Walk along the village street away from the Post Office and towards the church. Look for a pump on your right. Turn right immediately after it to pass Ty'n Llan on your left. Go ahead over a stile to follow a signposted public footpath. The enclosed path leads to a stile giving access to a field on your right. Bear left, crossing a track to reach a kissing-gate in the hedge ahead.

2. Go through the kissing-gate and continue across the next field to take another kissing-gate. Go ahead along the left-hand edge of the next field to a gate in its corner. Go through it and bear left to a farm (Marian).

3. Take the gate into the farmyard and continue along the farm access track. Shortly before this reaches the road, turn right along a roughly surfaced lane which leads to a bridge over the Afon Alaw.

4. Cross the bridge to reach Melin Hywel, a working water mill. Go ahead along its access lane to a road and turn right down to a bridge over the Afon Alaw again. Climb with the road up to Mount Alaw and go ahead to a crossroads. Maintain your direction to take the road to Melin Llynon, the windmill which appears on your right.

5. After visiting the windmill retrace your steps to the crossroads and turn left back to the village bus stop.

Public Transport

Come here on weekdays by bus no. 60 from Holyhead or Amlwch.

The Water Wheel at Melin Hywel (Howell's Mill) (Route 5)

Mynydd Bodafon

Outline

Maenaddwyn – Yr Arwydd – Maenaddwyn.

Summary

A quiet country lane links the bus stop with a rugged, windswept peak which offers fine views across the island and, even, to Ireland's Mountains of Mourne.

Attractions

Maenaddwyn's placename suggests that a standing stone is in the vicinity ('maen' means stone in Welsh). There is one beside the road running south from Maenaddwyn's crossroads, along the route taken by the no. 32 bus for Llangefni. It is at grid reference SH 461833. It is very tall and is recorded in one book as being 10 ft 6 in high. There may have been several stones here originally because the 1841 Ordnance Survey map marks the spot as Meini Addwyn ('meini' is stones, in the pleural).

This area certainly has a way of inspiring a respect for nature and history. Not far to the north, near Brynrefail, was the home of the remarkable Morris brothers. They helped make the 18th century the Age of Enlightenment. Lewis Morris (1701–65) was a surveyor, cartographer, historian and poet. Richard Morris (1703–79) made a collection of Anglesey's folksongs and started a cultural movement amongst the Welsh in London known as the Honourable Society of Cymmrodorion. William Morris (1705–63) was a famous botanist and gardener, while John Morris (1706–40) was a literary enthusiast who died fighting in Spain.

Most of Anglesey is a flat plateau, so a hill of over 500 feet can appear as impressive. The abrupt nature of the rocky outcrops here shows that older, harder, rocks have won through to survive the forces of erosion. The covering of gorse and heather suggests a rugged mountain, in contrast to the rolling green hills that can be seen all around. The highest point of Mynydd Bodafon is known as Yr Arwydd (the signal). Beacons must have been lit here in ancient times. They would have been seen from a vast area, as the view from the 583 ft summit is an excellent panorama.

As you look north, Holyhead Mountain is on your left, while the remains of Parys Mountain lie ahead. Mynydd Eilian is on the right of it. Look beyond these, however, on one of those special evenings that only a Celtic country can conjure up and you will see County Down's Mountains of Mourne sweeping down to the sea. The Isle of Man and the Lake District can also be made out as the sun sets on a day made clear by several hours of rain. Turn to the right to admire Snowdonia.

Refreshments

Bring your own sandwiches!

Route 6

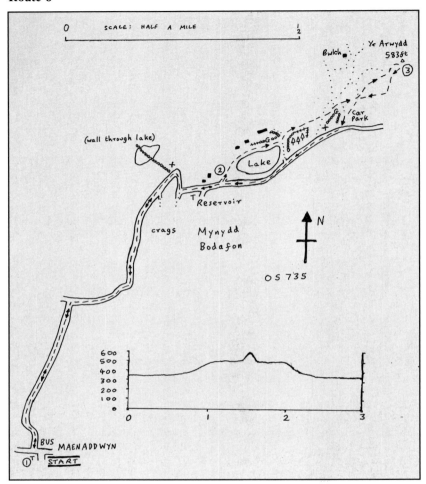

Route 6

Mynydd Bodafon
3 miles

Start

Maenaddwyn lies about 4 miles west of Benllech between the B5111 and the B5110. The crossroads at Maenaddwyn is a useful place to catch a bus. It also has a telephone box (GR SH 459841). A car park is marked on the map between the lake and Yr Arwydd.

Route

1. *Take the lane going away from the telephone box towards the rocky peak of Mynydd Bodafon. Go right at a T junction. Pass a chapel on the left below which is a small lake with a wall running through it. Immediately after the chapel, the lane bends sharply to the right.*

2. *In a short distance, bear left off the road along a track to pass a lake on your right. Go ahead past a plantation of trees on your right and across tracks to take the path ahead which climbs to the 583 ft summit of Yr Arwydd.*

3. *Descend and bear left to the road. Go right along it to pass the lake on your right and retrace your steps to the bus stop at Maenaddwyn.*

Public Transport

Bus no. 32 calls at Maenaddwyn on weekdays. This runs between Llangefni and Amlwch. Another weekday service is no. 63, running between Bangor and Amlwch. There is a no. 63 bus on Sundays but it takes the coastal route and doesn't stop here.

Admire the view from the 583 ft summit of Yr Arwydd

The Dove Cote, Penmon Priory (Route 7)

Penmon Priory

Outline
Bus Stop at T Junction – Penmon – Penmon Priory – Bus Stop.

Summary
Climb lanes to where the fieldpaths afford a view of Puffin Island (the small one to the north, not the bulk of the Great Orme that can be seen away to the east). Visit an Augustinian Priory and descend to the shore of the Menai Strait on the way back to the bus stop.

Attractions
Penmon is one of Anglesey's holiest spots. Tradition states that a priory was founded here in about 540, during the reign of Maelgwn Gwynedd. The founder may have been Cynlas but his brother and successor Seiriol is most associated with this place. A member of Gwynedd's royal family, he chose the life of a monk and baptised converts in the holy well that bears his name. He probably lived in the nearby cell whose outline survives. A contemporary of Holyhead's St Cybi, Seiriol used to walk halfway across the island each week to meet Cybi at Llanerchymedd. As he walked westward in the morning and eastward later in the day he always had the sun on his back and remained pale, becoming known as Seiriol the Fair. Cybi had the benefit of the sun both ways and was known as the Dark.

Viking raids during the 10th century wiped away traces of the Celtic monastic community but the present church was built in the 12th century and the community adopted the Augustinian rule. The Penmon Cross is now located in the nave of the church, to the left of the entrance. It originally stood nearby in what became Penmon deer park. The Bulkeley family gained possession of the property and built the dovecote. About 1000 pigeons were kept here as a source of fresh meat during the winter. The south range of the monastic buildings are on the other side of the road from the dovecote, immediately after the church. The three-storey building dates from the 13th century and comprised a dormitory, a dining room and a cellar. A new block was added near the present road in the 16th century. It has a fireplace at ground level, indicating how the monks had grown soft! Another fireplace was in the kitchen on the first floor. The prior's house is still lived in.

The Rev. Elias Owen recorded a cure from the 19th century that had taken place at St Seiriol's holy well. It was told him by a gentleman farmer who had gone to the well at midnight to fetch water for a friend who was on the point of death. The sick man drank the water, revived and lived to enjoy forty more years of life in perfect health. Modern research is showing that holy wells do have special properties.

The whale-backed shape of Puffin Island can be seen from this walk. It is 1200 yards long, 400 yards wide and rises to 200 feet in height. The sound that separates it

Continued on page 38

Route 7

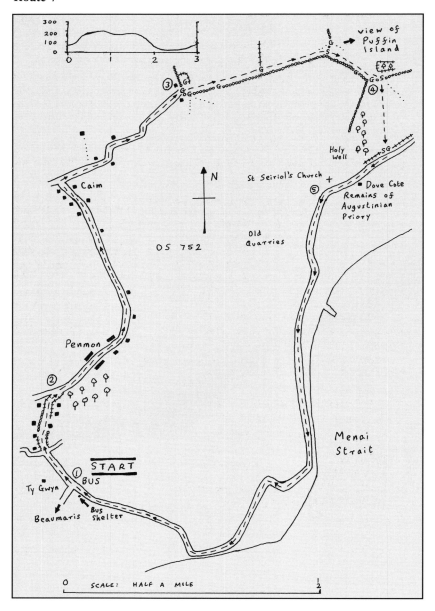

view of Puffin Island

300
200
100
0

③ G

G

St Seiriol's Church

Holy Well

GoS ④

SG

⑤

Dove Cote
Remains of
Augustinian
Priory

Caim

OS 752

Old Quarries

N

Penmon

②

Menai Strait

① START
BUS

Ty Gwyn

Beaumaris   Bus Shelter

0   SCALE: HALF A MILE   ½

Route 7

Penmon Priory

3 miles

Start

Cars may be parked near Penmon Priory. Penmon is on the eastern tip of Anglesey 4 miles north of Beaumaris. The walk is described from the bus stop at the T-junction below Penmon. This has a shelter near it, on the turning for the Menai Strait (GR SH 622797).

Route

1. Face the bus timetable at the T-junction and go left, soon passing Ty Gwyn on your left. Reach a road junction and go straight ahead up a footpath which climbs past houses.

2. Bear right along the road through Penmon to Caim. Turn right at the T-junction here to follow a No Through Road.

3. When the road ends, go ahead through a gate and walk along the right-hand edge of a field, beside a high wall on your right. Go ahead through a gate and continue to a ladder stile in the corner of the next field. Bear right, as waymarked, over it. Walk beside a wall on your right and notice Puffin Island away to your left.

4. Cross the stone step stile in the wall and ignore the waymarked path bearing left by going straight ahead down to a stile beside a gate. This gives access to a road. Go right down it to see the dovecote on your left and St Seiriol's church on your right. A path opposite the dovecote goes round the wall of the graveyard and past the monk's fishpond to St Seiriol's cell and holy well.

5. After visiting the ruins of Penmon Priory go down the road to the seashore and follow it inland to return to the bus stop.

Public Transport

There is a daily bus service (no. 57) to the start of this walk from Bangor via Beaumaris. Why not leave your car in the car park at Beaumaris and come here by bus? The service is surprisingly good (hourly on weekdays) and these lanes weren't meant for cars.

from Anglesey is 800 yards wide and this was enough to isolate it as a home for hermits. Its Welsh name is Ynys Seiriol, the island of the saint who was at Penmon. They weren't left in peace, however. As early as 632 there is a record of the Saxon Edwin, King of Northumbria, besieging Cadwallon, King of Gwynedd, on the island. The Vikings came in the 10th century but by the 12th the hermits were back on a large scale. There were so many that arguments were common. These led to a plague of mice, who were known to disappear as soon as the arguments were over. The hermits have now gone but the place is infested with rats. They have even virtually eliminated the population of puffins that gave the island its English name. Humans did their best to keep the puffins' numbers down until this century. Recipes exist for making puffin flesh pallatable (the birds' usual diet was sand-eels). Puffins were filleted, their oil was extracted and their flesh was marinated in spices and vinegar. Barrel loads of them were exported to England and France, suggesting that people must have been really hungry in those days! Boat trips around the island can be booked from Beaumaris and Llandudno (on the mainland). You could travel between Llandudno and Puffin Island by road in the 5th century. The Menai Strait was narrow then and Puffin Island was on the eastern side. Sea now covers the recorded territory of Tyno Helig or Helig's Vale. Its capital was Llys Helig, located north of Penmaenmawr.

Refreshments
Bring your own sandwiches!

Llyn Maelog, Rhosneigr (Route 8)

Llyn Maelog

Outline

Rhosneigr – Llyn Maelog – Rhosneigr.

Summary

Bird-watchers will love this walk around a lake fringed by beds of reeds. Allow time to relax on the beach at Rhosneigr.

Attractions

This has become a very anglicised area, having attracted English people to retire here, being popular with English holidaymakers and near RAF Valley. Surfing is a favourite pursuit in the bay, while there is also a golf course. In the 18th century this was a desolate area, however, as reflected in the placename (Rhos = moor, y Neidr = of the adder). A notorious gang of wreckers lured ships ashore on the nearby beach (Traeth Crigyll), waving lanterns at night. Caught and condemned to be hanged at Beaumaris Assizes in 1741, their story is the subject of a ballad entitled 'Crogi Lladron Crigyll' (The hanging of the thieves of Crigyll) composed by Lewis Morris (of the family featured in route 6).

Llyn Maelog is a large lake which becomes home for waders in winter, when you may spot great crested grebe, little grebe, heron, greylag goose, wigeon, gadwall, teal, mallard, shoveler, pochard, tufted duck, goldeneye, red-breasted mergenser, coot, oystercatcher, golden plover, lapwing, snipe, curlew and redshank. In the summer you can see little grebe, great crested grebe, mute swan, greylag goose, shelduck, pochard, tufted duck, ruddy duck, red-breasted merganser, black-headed gull, grey partridge, stonechat, sedge warbler, reed warbler, whitethroat and reed bunting.

Just over 1 mile away, on the other side of the railway, near Llanfaelog, at grid reference SH 344738, is Ty Newydd Burial Chamber. Probably dating from the New Stone Age, pottery and a flint arrowhead of early Bronze Age date have been found here. A large damaged capstone, 12 feet by 5 feet, covers uprights which are now supplemented by two modern pillars. A round cairn probably covered the monument originally.

Drama came to Cymyran Bay, north of Rhosneigr, on 29 March 1883. The *Norman Court*, a rigged barque of 855 tons from Greenock, was sailing home with a cargo of sugar from Java when a gale forced her ashore on Cymyran Beach. The Rhosneigr lifeboat went to the rescue but was soon incapacitated. The Holyhead lifeboat similarly failed in several valiant attempts to reach her. Eventually the Holyhead Crew used the Rhosneigr lifeboat to rescue 20 people, with two more dead from hypothermia.

Route 8

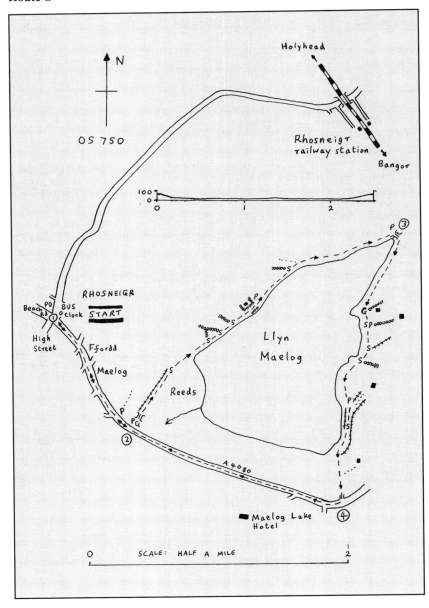

40

Route 8

Llyn Maelog

$2\frac{1}{2}$ **miles**

Start
From the clock opposite the Post Office in Rhosneigr. This is where buses stop. Park considerately nearby (GR SH 319732).

Route
1. Face the Post Office and turn sharply left along Ffordd Maelog. Ignore the first signposted public footpath that you come to on your left.

2. Turn left through a gate and over a footbridge to follow a signposted public footpath. Pass beds of reeds on your right and walk beside a fence on your left. Continue over a series of stiles and with the lake on your right.

3. Cross the footbridge at the neck of the lake and turn sharply right to walk with the lake still on your right. Go ahead over a series of stiles and emerge along a track to join the main road.

4. Go right along the wide verge to pass Maelog Lake Hotel on your left. Retrace your steps into Rhosneigr.

Public Transport
Come here by train, although the station is a mile from the start of the walk (just follow the road into the village, as shown on the map). Bus no. 45 links Rhosneigr on weekdays with Llangefni and Holyhead.

Refreshments
There is a cafe as well as shops in Rhosneigr.

41

The Dingle, Llangefni

Llangefni

Outline

Llangefni – The Dingle – Llangefni.

Summary

This is a pleasant, relaxing, walk beside a river and through mature deciduous woodland to meadows. A brief climb leads to the road back down to Llangefni.

Attractions

Until 1760 this was the furthest navigable point up the Afon Cefni. Its central location has made it the administrative capital of the island. The town hall stands near the clock tower, built to commemorate the Boer War. Megan Lloyd George was elected as an MP here in 1945. In 1992, the member for Anglesey was Ieuan Wyn Jones (Plaid Cymru).

Llangefni is a busy market town, with stalls on Thursdays throughout the year plus Saturdays in the summer. The large livestock market (opposite the turning for the church) operates on Wednesdays. The stone tower of St Cyngar's church has a fine backdrop of woodland. The building was rebuilt in 1824 but there is a 5th century gravestone and a 12th century font. The nearby picnic place is the start of the Dingle, where a peaceful path through the oak and beech woods provides shelter and, perhaps, glimpses of sparrowhawk, kestrel, tawny owl, stock dove, coal tit, treecreeper, blackcap, sedge warbler and other birds.

The walk back along the pavement of the road passes the modern Plas Arthur Leisure Centre. Here you can swim in a heated pool, play squash or badminton, climb a special wall and purchase refreshments in the cafe. Sadly, Llangefni's railway station is closed, but the line to Amlwch remains open for freight traffic.

Llangefni has had a stirring, enthusiastic, approach to religion. John Elias, the Calvinistic Methodist, used to preach here in the early 19th century, while Penuel Baptist chapel commemorates Christmas Evans, a great preacher and hymn-writer who settled in the town in 1791.

Refreshments

Plenty of choice in Llangefni!

Route 9

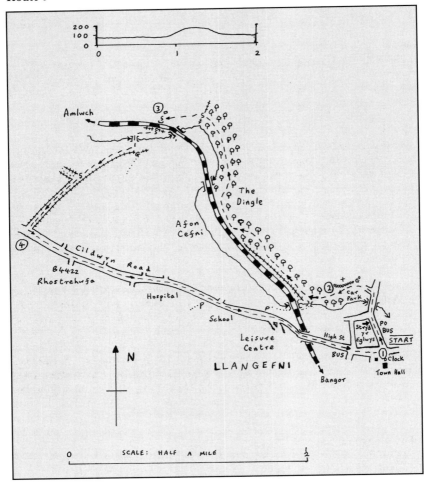

Amlwch

The
Dingle

Afon
Cefni

Cildwrn   Road

B4422
Rhostrehwfa

Hospital

School

Leisure
Centre

LLANGEFNI

Bangor

High St

Stryd
yr
Eglwys

car
Park

PO
BUS

START

BUS

O'Clock

Town Hall

N

SCALE: HALF A MILE

Route 9

Llangefni

2 miles

Start

Buses going from Bangor to Holyhead stop in the High Street but buses going from Holyhead to Bangor and other routes stop near the Post Office in Strydyr Eglwys. The clock tower is a convenient central point (GR SH 459757). There is a car-park near the church (point 2).

Route

1. Cross the road carefully to walk away from the clock tower and up Strydyr Eglwys, passing the Post Office on your right. Continue over the bridge across the Afon Cefni. Pass the livestock market on your right and turn left to the church, where there is a car-park and picnic area.

2. With the church on your right and the river on your left, go ahead along the path through the Dingle, ignoring a footbridge on your left. Emerge over a stile and bear left to pass a ruin on your right and cross a stile giving access to a tunnel under the railway.

3. Emerge over another stile from under the railway and bear right. Turn left to cross a footbridge over the river and climb the slope ahead. Do not go through a gate ahead but turn right to walk with a hedge on your left and above the valley on your right. Continue along an enclosed track to the main road.

4. Turn left along the pavement of the road back to Llangefni. The leisure centre will appear on your right, after the hospital and the school but before the bridge across the railway. Notice a ruined windmill on the skyline ahead of you as you enter the town.

Public Transport

A host of buses stop in Llangefni. No. 4 runs on weekdays between Bangor and Holyhead, with no. 44 providing a daily service, no. 32 runs to and from Amlwch on weekdays, no. 44 provides a weekday service between Llangefni and Bangor via Newborough, no. 45 runs on weekdays to and from Holyhead via Rhosneigr, no. 50 runs on Thursdays from Amlwch via Benllech, no. 51 runs on Thursdays from Beaumaris via Benllech, no. 55 is an infrequent weekday service from Newborough, no. 70 operates on Thursdays from Llanrhyddlad and no. 232 runs from Amlwch via Cemaes on Thursdays. It's obvious on which day you should plan your trip here!

Beaumaris Castle

Beaumaris Castle

Outline
Beaumaris Castle – Site of Franciscan Monastery – Beaumaris Castle.

Summary
Most of this walk is along a quiet lane which provides splendid views of the castle and of the mountains of Snowdonia. The final section follows a fieldpath above the Menai Strait.

Attractions
You can't come to Wales and not visit a castle! Beaumaris has one of the best. It is, of course, a reminder of how the English subjugated the Welsh and the fact that such an impressive fortress was required bears witness to the national spirit surviving in this part of Wales. Construction began in 1295 and the design was on the concentric plan. An outer moat protected a narrow enclosing ward which surrounded the main courtyard of the castle. Beaumaris displays perfect symmetry, achieved because of its level, marshy, site. It lacks the high towers of other castles, however, and seems disappointing when seen from ground level at close quarters. This walk brings a much better view of it.

The lack of towers, which weren't built because the money (millions of pounds in modern terms) ran out, didn't really matter in the end as the defences were never put to a test. It was originally built to protect the town of Llanfaes, the island's chief trading town and the home of a Franciscan Monastery, within whose church lay buried Joan, the daughter of King John and the wife of Llywelyn the Great. It held a strategic position on the route to Ireland via Holyhead. It became the centre for the English administration of Anglesey. Its name betrays its Norman conception, meaning 'fair marsh' (Norman-French 'Beau Mareys'). The local Welsh population was ethnically cleansed to Newborough, 12 miles away.

Never actually completed, the money wasn't found to maintain it and by 1534 'there was scarcely a single chamber in Beaumaris Castle where a man could lie dry'. A report of 1539 stated that the castle was left with no guns or powder 'apart from eight or ten small pieces . . . possessed by the writer (Sir Richard Bulkeley) has provided three barrels of gunpowder, some shot, forty bows, forty sheaves of arrows, with as many coats of fence and sallets and splinters, at his own cost; this is inadequate for such a fortress.'

Now in the care of Cadw (Heritage in Wales), the castle is open daily except over Christmas. The Museum of Childhood (tel. 0248 712498) is nearby.

Refreshments
Refreshments are available in Beaumaris.

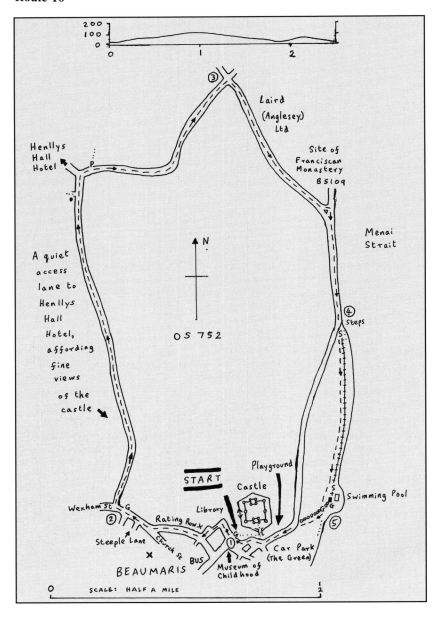

START

Castle

Playground

Library

Museum of Childhood

BEAUMARIS

Wexham St.

Rating Row

Steeple Lane

Church St.

BUS

Car Park (The Green)

Swimming Pool

Henllys Hall Hotel

Laird (Anglesey) Ltd

Site of Franciscan Monastery B5109

Menai Strait

N

OS 752

A quiet access lane to Henllys Hall Hotel, affording fine views of the castle

Steps

SCALE: HALF A MILE

Route 10

Beaumaris Castle

$2\frac{1}{2}$ miles

Start

The entrance to Beaumaris Castle is convenient for cars parked on The Green and for the bus stops in Castle Street (GR SH 606762).

Route

1. Face Beaumaris Castle and go left to pass the library on your right. Turn right along Rating Row and keep right at Church Street.

2. Turn right up the lane signposted as the access to Henllys Hall Hotel. Look back for a fine view of Beaumaris Castle, on your right. Turn right with the lane when the access drive to the hotel bears left. Admire Snowdonia, across the Menai Strait, ahead.

3. At the crossroads, turn right to pass Laird (Anglesey) Ltd and the site of a Franciscan Monastery on your left. Join the B5109 and turn right along its pavement to walk beside the sea wall on your left.

4. When the road veers inland, go ahead up steps and walk above the road to an iron ladder stile. Cross it to enter the corner of a field. Go ahead along the seaward edge of the field. Descend to a kissing-gate in the corner of a wall ahead.

5. Go through the kissing-gate and follow the wall on your right to reach the road. Go left along its pavement to pass a children's playground just before Beaumaris Castle on your right.

Public Transport

Bus no. 51 runs from Llangefni to Beaumaris on Thursdays, the no. 53 service between Bangor and Llanddona stops in Beaumaris on weekdays (early departures from Bangor are numbered 56), while there is a good daily service from Bangor to Penmon via Beaumaris (no. 57).

On the path south of Aberffraw

Aberffraw

Outline
Aberffraw – Penrhyn-du – Aberffraw.

Summary
Walk south from the old royal seat of power in Gwynedd by following the river towards the sea. Turn inland along firm tracks to reach a quiet lane which affords a view over an old coastal church and leads past the site of the old palace before entering the village.

Attractions
Matholwch, King of Ireland came to Wales to ask for the hand of Branwen, daughter of Llyr (Shakespeare's King Lear and the legendary founder of London). Acclaimed in *The Mabinogion* as the 'fairest maiden in the world', she met her suitor at Aberffraw, where 'they began the feast and sat them down'. Significantly, 'they were not within a house, but within tents . . . and that night Matholwch slept with Branwen'.

Here we have proof that Aberffraw was the royal seat in ancient times. We also have the reason why only a few shards of pottery survive as material evidence. Even when the Welsh princes stopped living in tents, their palace was built of wood. Wood was the Celtic medium and available in plentiful supply. The independent princes of Gwynedd ruled from here until Llywelyn the Last's death in 1282. There were other royal houses and forts (Maelgwn Gwynedd favoured Deganwy, near Llandudno) but this is the authentic spot. Yet there is little to see at Aberffraw today. Come here for a sense of glorious memories and spiritial association with the past and rightful rulers. The old wooden palace actually stood in a field passed on your right as you return to the village. It survived Edward I's invasion and the loss of Welsh independence but was demolished in 1317. Its timbers were needed in the final stage of construction of Caernarfon Castle.

One place you can learn about Aberffraw's history is the Coastal Heritage Centre at Llys Llywelyn, near the Prince Llywelyn pub at the northern end of the village. There is an audio-visual centre and exhibitions on the natural environment. The work of the famous bird artist C. F. Tunnicliffe, who lived locally, is on display, while refreshments are available in the cafe. This Centre is open daily in the summer from 11 am to 5.30 pm (tel. 0407 840845).

Pilgrimages used to be made to St Cwyfan's church, which now has just the annual service in late May or early June. St Cwyfan came here to pray in the 7th century. He was a follower of St Beuno.

Refreshments
Refreshments are available in Aberffraw.

Route 11

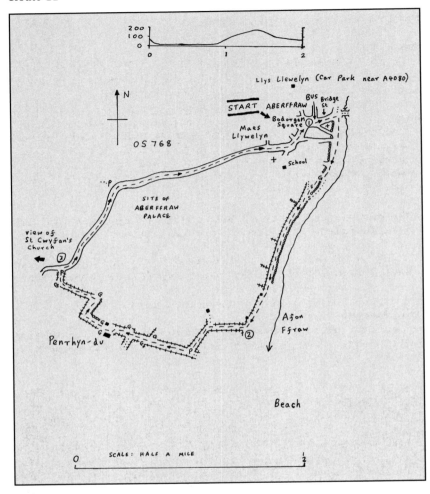

Route 11

Aberffraw

2 miles

Start

Aberffraw is about 16 miles west of Menai Bridge on the A4080. Start at Bodorgan Square in the centre of the village, where the buses stop. Park cars considerately here or at Llys Llewelyn (near the A4080) (GR SH 355689).

Route

1. Standing in Bodorgan Square (Sgwar Bodorgan), face The Crown Inn (Y Goron) and go left down towards the river (Afon Aberffraw), passing the Methodist chapel on your right. Don't take the bridge across the river. Turn right along the track which runs beside the river, now flowing towards the sea on your left. Go ahead for half a mile.

2. Turn right along a hedged track. Go left at a junction with another track and reach a signposted junction. Turn right to follow a track to a lane.

3. When you reach the lane notice the view over St Cwyfan's church on the coast to your left. Continue this walk by turning right along the lane back to Aberffraw.

Public Transport

Bus no. 42 provides a service on weekdays between Bangor and Llangefni via Aberffraw. There is also a weekday service between Holyhead and Llangefni via Aberffraw (no. 45).

'Llwybr Cyhoeddus' means public footpath in Welsh

53

Ynys Llanddwyn (Route 16)

Llyn Coron

Outline

Bodorgan Railway Station – Llyn Coron – Llangadwaladr – Bodorgan
Railway Station.

Summary

A lane, track and fieldpaths lead from the station to a lake which is a favourite with
bird watchers. Climb to the old church at Llangadwaladr before returning to the
station.

Attractions

The station may be named Bodorgan but that place is actually south of this walk.
The name appealed because of the great house and estate at Bodorgan. It was the
home of Owen Meyrick who, as Anglesey's MP from 1715 to 1722, assisted the
career of Lewis Morris and his brothers (see route 6).

Llyn Coron is the large lake near the station and bird watchers resort to it. In the
summer you can see great crested grebe, little grebe, mute swan, shelduck, shoveler,
ruddy duck, coot, moorhen, oystercatcher, curlew, redshank, grey partridge, red-
legged partridge, barn owl, little owl, grasshopper warbler, sedge warbler,
whitethroat, stonechat, yellowhammer and redpoll. In the winter look out for great
crested grebe, little grebe, heron, mute swan, whooper swan, greylag goose, white-
fronted goose, Canada goose, ruddy duck, wigeon, teal, mallard, pintail, shoveler,
pochard, tufted duck, goldeneye, water rail, coot, oystercatcher, golden plover,
lapwing, snipe and curlew.

Llangadwaladr's church is dedicated to the saintly king who was the last British
ruler to claim jurisdiction over all of the island of Britain, in the 7th century. As
Bretwalda he also represented the Saxon areas. About 1000 years were to elapse
before Britain was united again. Some of the Welsh princes, whose court at
Aberffraw was nearby, were buried here. A 7th century inscribed stone was placed
by Cadwaladr. It describes his grandfather, Cadfan, as the 'wisest and most
illustrious of kings'. St Cadwaladr himself is portrayed in a window dating from the
15th century. The Owen Chapel, erected in Llangadwaladr's church by his widow
Ann in 1660, suggests that Col. Hugh Owen fought gallantly for the royalist cause.
In fact he preferred not to get involved.

Refreshments

Bring your own sandwiches!

Route 12

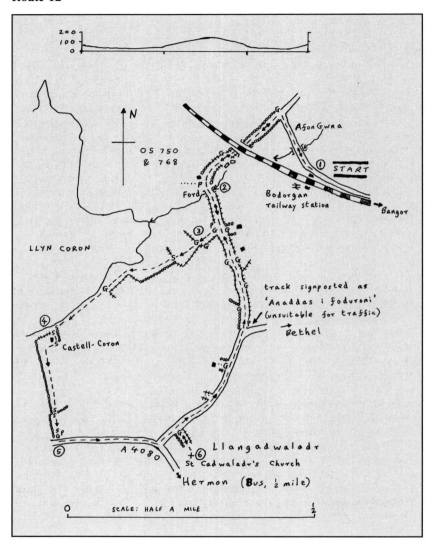

200
100
0

↑ N

OS 750 & 768

AfonGwna

① START

Bodorgan railway station

→ Bangor

Ford

②

P

③

LLYN CORON

S

track signposted as 'Anaddas i foduroni' (unsuitable for traffic)

→ Bethel

④

Castell-Coron

⑤   A 4080

+⑥ Llangadwaladr
St Cadwaladr's Church

→ Hermon (Bus, ½ mile)

O   SCALE: HALF A MILE   ½

56

Route 12

Llyn Coron

$2\frac{3}{4}$ miles

Start

The walk starts at Bodorgan Station which lies about 14 miles west of Menai Bridge and 2 miles east of Aberffraw near the junction of the B4422 with the A4080. Come here by train. Bodorgan is a request halt on the railway between Bangor and Holyhead (GR SH 387702).

Route

1. *With your back to the railway station, go left up the road until it bends right. Turn left here along a track which leads under the railway and past ruined farm buildings on your left. Ignore a signposted public footpath which bears right. Cross a river (Afon Gwna) by a footbridge next to the ford.*

2. *Go ahead until there is a public footpath signpost beside a gate on your right, opposite a gate to a house on your left. Go into the field to follow the path to a kissing-gate ahead, ignoring a gate on your left.*

3. *Cross the next field to a stile and continue towards the lake. Walk through another kissing-gate and with the lake on your right to a wooden step stile. Cross this and immediately turn left to go over a stone stile.*

4. *Walk past a house (Castell-Coron) on your right, away from Llyn Coron. Continue along the right-hand edge of a field, cross a double stile in its far corner and go ahead to a road, which is reached by crossing a stile and taking a kissing-gate beside a public footpath signpost.*

5. *Turn left along the road's wide verge. Fork left at Llangadwaladr, along the road signposted as going to Bethel. Take a small gate on your right to divert up the enclosed concrete path to the old church.*

6. *Retrace your steps to the road and go right to resume your former direction. When the road bears right, go straight ahead down a track signposted as being 'unsuitable for traffic' (anaddas i foduroni). This leads back to where you took the signposted footpath through a kissing-gate on your outward journey. Retrace your steps over the footbridge beside the ford and back to Bodorgan railway station.*

Public Transport

Trains stop by request at Bodorgan (daily service). Buses 42 (Llangefni–Bangor) and 45 (Holyhead–Llangefni) stop in Hermon, half a mile east along the A4080 from Llangadwaladr, on weekdays.

The entrance to Bryn Celli Ddu Burial Chamber

Bryn Celli Ddu

Outline
Llanddaniel Fab – Bryn Celli Ddu – Llanddaniel Fab.

Summary
This is a simple, linear, walk from the nearest bus stop to one of Anglesey's most important ancient monuments.

Attractions
Llanddaniel Fab means 'Church of Deiniol the patron saint'. It is a parish which has witnessed history and prehistory. We may assume that it is where the historical event of the Roman invasion of Anglesey took place because a field in the parish is still called 'Maes Mawr y Gad' (Field of the Great Army) and tradition insists the Romans wiped out the druids here. Druidism was the old religion of the Celts, who settled in Britain around 500 BC, in the Iron Age. The Gauls, in modern France, looked to Britain for support when they were attacked by the Romans because Druidism was based here, on Anglesey. When the Roman empire extended itself to include Britain it became necessary, as Tacitus recorded, 'to attack the island of Anglesey, which was feeding the native resistance'.

So, in 61 AD, the Roman general Suetonius Paulinus arrived on the shore of the Menai Strait with two legions. Including mercenaries and cavalry, he had at least 10,000 men. They hesitated before crossing to the sacred island, however, as Tacitus recounts: 'By the shore stood an opposing battle-line, thick with men and weapons, women running between them, like the Furies in their funereal clothes, their hair flowing, carrying torches; and druids among them, pouring out frightful curses with their hands raised high to the heavens, our soldiers being so scared by the unfamiliar sight that their limbs were paralysed, and they stood motionless and exposed to be wounded.'

Suetonius Paulinus managed to inspire his men to cross, using a flotilla of flat-bottomed boats brought from Chester and encouraging the horses to swim (indicating that it was an easier crossing in those days). Roman propaganda makes much of how bloodthirsty the druids were, but they actually practised pacifism and offered no resistance. Indeed, as the old religion was being destroyed on Anglesey, the druids down in Somerset were becoming the first Christians, worshipping at the church that Jesus had built in Glastonbury. Jesus was the expected Messiah of the druids, being their god Esse and He had spent a winter in Somerset as a youth with his tin-trader great-uncle Joseph of Arimathea. Joseph returned to Glastonbury with Mary, the mother of Jesus, around 61 AD. The British King Lucius made Christianity his state religion around 160 AD.

There are 2000 years between us and the druids. Similarly, there were 2000 years

Continued on page 62

Route 13

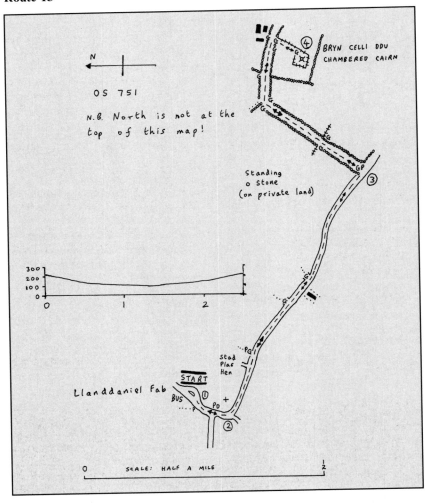

N

OS 751

N.B. North is not at the top of this map!

BRYN CELLI DDU CHAMBERED CAIRN

④

Standing o Stone (on private land)

③

Stad Plas Hen

START

Llanddaniel Fab

BUS

①

②

SCALE: HALF A MILE

60

Route 13

Bryn Celli Ddu

$2\frac{1}{2}$ miles

Start

The walk starts at Llanddaniel Fab, between the A5 and the A4080 three miles west of Llanfair P.G. Cars may be parked in a lay-by near the bus stop in Llanddaniel Fab (GR SH 496706).

Route

1. *Go to the village Post Office, at the head of a T-junction. Walk past the Post Office on your left, ignoring the road on your right.*

2. *Turn left along the road signposted as being for Llanedwen. Pass a church on your left. Continue down the road, passing the road for Stad Plas Hen on your left.*

3. *Turn left at a track signposted as being for Bryn Celli Ddu Burial Chamber. Follow this track as it bends right. Reach a small gate giving access to the field containing the burial chamber. Turn right and walk beside a fence on your left to the ancient monument.*

4. *Retrace your steps back to the bus stop in Llanddaniel Fab.*

Public Transport

About half of the no. 4 buses running between Bangor and Holyhead go via Llanddaniel Fab on weekdays, giving an hourly service.

61

between the druids and the builders of Bryn Celli Ddu Burial Chamber. It is so old that we know hardly anything about it. Excavations do show that there was a henge, with a stone circle surrounded by a bank and internal ditch. The burial chamber was then imposed on this. Some say that this represents a victory for an older religion over the new. The mound with its passage grave is certainly typical of the New Stone Age. Inside is (or was, the original stone is now in the National Museum of Wales, Cardiff, with a replica here) a stone decorated with a spiral and wavy lines. Similar patterns are seen at New Grange in Ireland and in Brittany. Such things are fascinating and open to all sorts of explanations. Much solid work is being done on the subject, however, including the significance of these sites being on ley lines or spirit paths. Carmel Head, on the island's north coast at grid reference SH 295930 may also be of significance. Keep up to date on this subject by reading *The Ley Hunter*, the international magazine of leys and Earth Mysteries (39 Alma Place, Penzance, Cornwall, TR18 2BX).

Refreshments
There is a shop in Llanddaniel Fab.

Can you say it?

$1\frac{1}{2}$ miles

Llanfairpwllgwyngyllgogerychwyrndrobwllllantysiliogogogoch

Outline

Railway Station – Marquess of Anglesey's Column – Railway Station.

Summary

You can't come to Anglesey and miss the place with the longest name! Neither should you miss the joy of climbing up the Marquess of Anglesey's Column to admire the view. This walk joins the two.

Attractions

A clever piece of marketing by a local businessman created the name of this place, which translates as 'St Mary's church in a hollow by the white hazel close to the rapid whirlpool by the red cave of St Tysilio'. St Mary's church is here, while St Tysilio's church is at the foot of a steep lane, by the shores of the Menai Strait, where there are whirlpools. The red cave has been lost, however, while the white hazels are now oaks.

The village saw the first ever meeting of the Women's Institute in Great Britain in 1915. A Canadian visitor (the W.I. started in Canada in 1897) suggested it and the initial meeting was held in Yr Hafoty. In 1921 the W.I. moved to a new building next to the Tollhouse (this was the last surviving public toll road in 1895). Ironically, Welsh-speaking women now tend to join the Merched y Wawr, a Welsh-speaking movement for women founded at Bala in 1967.

The Marquess of Anglesey, then the Earl of Uxbridge and formerly Lord Paget, was in charge of the cavalry and second in command of the British forces at the Battle of Waterloo in 1815. He made the famous remark during the battle to the Duke of Wellington, 'By God sir, I've lost my leg!' 'By God sir, you have!', replied the duke. He lost a leg but gained a 91 feet high fluted Tuscan column with an internal spiral staircase of 115 steps climbing to an open parapet surrounding the pedestal on which the statue of the marquess stands. The column was erected in 1816 but the statue didn't surmount it until 1860. The inscription on the base of the column gives the date of the Battle of Waterloo as 16 June 1815, when it was actually 18 June.

From the top of the tower look for the Nelson Monument near the Britannia Bridge. This railway bridge was built by Robert Stephenson between 1845 and 1850. A fire in 1970 caused its closure for two years and it now carries the A5 road above the railway. The station at the start of this walk was, incredibly, closed in 1965 but reopened in 1973.

Refreshments

There are several shops near the start of this walk.

Route 14

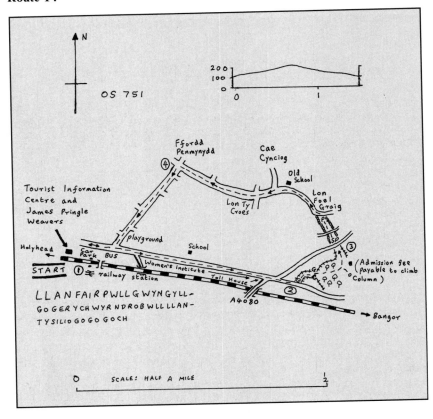

Route 14

Llanfairpwllgwyngyllgogerychwyrndrobwllllantysiliogogogoch $1\frac{1}{2}$ miles

Start

> There is a car-park and a bus stop near the British Rail station at Llan-fairpwllgwyngyllgogerychwyrndrobwllllantysiliogogogoch (GR SH 526716).

Route

1. With the Tourist Information Centre and James Pringle Weavers on your left, go right to follow the pavement of the Holyhead Road, in the direction of Menai Bridge. Pass a school on your left. At a junction, notice the first Women's Institute in Great Britain and the old Tollhouse on your right. Go ahead past a bus stop.

2. Turn left through a car-park and go up the path to the Marquess of Anglesey's Column, where you can pay a fee to climb the 115 steps to a viewing gallery. Continue by bearing left with the footpath to a road.

3. Cross the road and take the signposted enclosed footpath which goes over the stile ahead. Cross a lane and reach another road (Lon Foel Graig). Turn left along this to pass the old school on your right. Keep straight ahead at Lon Ty Croes.

4. Turn left at Ffordd Penmynydd and return to Holyhead Road, passing the surgery and children's swings on your left. Cross the Holyhead Road and go right to return to the Tourist Information Centre and the station.

Public Transport

Llanfairpwllgwyngyllgogerychwyrndrobwllllantysiliogogogoch is a request halt on the railway line between Bangor and Holyhead. Bus no. 4 stops here on its way between Bangor and Holyhead on weekdays – it's no. 44 on Sundays. Bus no. 43 between Bangor and Malltraeth also stops here on weekdays.

The Menai Suspension Bridge

Menai Bridge

Outline

Public Library – Coed Cyrnol – Belgian Promenade – Menai Suspension Bridge – Love Lane – Public Library.

Summary

This is a delightful little walk through woodland and beside the Menai Strait. Admire the famous bridge and pass a Gorsedd stone circle.

Attractions

Ferries crossed the Menai Strait from here, while livestock were sold at an annual fair (Ffair y Borth is still held at the end of each October), then swum across to the mainland, for centuries before a bridge was built. The long wait resulted in the world's first large iron suspension bridge being built by Thomas Telford and opened to traffic in January, 1826. It had to allow sailing ships a clear passage at high water, so it is 100 feet above high water mark.

One of the best views of the bridge can be had from Church Island. St Tysilio built the first church here in 630, while the present building dates from the 13th century. Giraldus Cambrensis and Archbishop Baldwin probably preached the crusade in 1188 here, although none of the assembled Welsh knights volunteered their services. A hoard of Roman coins dating from 268 AD was found in Coed Cyrnol, now covered in Scots pine and oak. Belgian refugees built and gave their name to the promenade during World War I. It makes a fine observation platform for seeing birds on the mud flats. In the woods near the bridge is a Gorsedd stone circle. It seems too neatly arranged to have been erected in the early Bronze Age. In fact it was placed here for the 1963 National Eisteddfod.

The Gorsedd (meaning throne) was a ritual concocted by Edward Williams, a Welsh stonemason living in London. He was a long distance walker, a poet, an antiquarian, a laudanum addict and a man who looked forward to the replacement of Christianity by the old druid religion. Believing that the Mandan Indians in America were of Welsh descent, he intended to put his ideals into practice with a community in the New World. Under his bardic name of Iolo Morgannwg he purported to write about unbroken traditions, such as 'Gorsedd Beirdd Ynys Prydain' (The Gorsedd of the Bards of Britain) when these ceremonies were the product of his own fertile imagination. Eisteddfod organisers accepted Iolo's evidence of druidical ceremonial and regalia, probably dating only from 1792 when Iolo first put on a show at Primrose Hill, London. Never mind, it's all colourful fun and Iolo was extremely gifted and energetic in his own way.

Refreshments

Refreshments are available in Menai Bridge.

Route 15

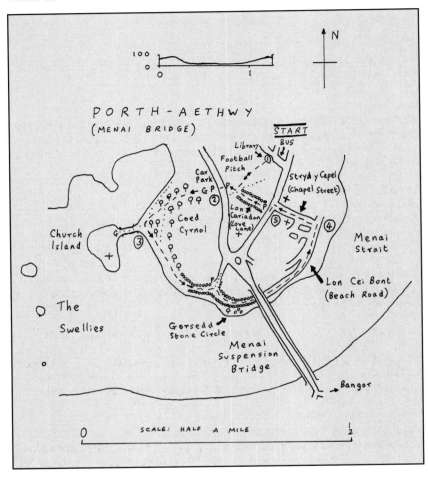

Route 15

Menai Bridge

$1\frac{1}{4}$ miles

Start

The walk is described from the Public Library at Menai Bridge, near the bus stops (GR SH 556720).

Route

1. Take the path running behind the library and following the edge of woodland on your left, overlooking a football pitch on your right. Climb to a path junction and bear right to a kissing-gate beside a public footpath signpost. Go ahead over the road with care.

2. Continue along a signposted public footpath, passing a Chinese restaurant on your left and a car-park on your right. Enter woodland (Coed Cyrnol) and follow what is known as the Belgian Promenade down to the bridge for Church Island.

3. Walk along the promenade at the foot of woodland on your left, with the sea wall on your right. Notice the Britannia Bridge away to your right. Climb to a path junction and ignore the path which bears left. Go ahead past the Gorsedd stone circle shaded by trees on your right. Pass under an arch of the Menai Suspension Bridge and continue along Lon Cei Bont (Beach Road).

4. Turn left up Stryd y Capel (Chapel Street). At the top, go left a few paces.

5. Cross the road carefully to take the kissing-gate beside a public footpath signpost and follow Lon Cariadon (Love Lane). Emerge at the path junction above the football pitch and bear right on the path back down to the library and bus stops.

Public Transport

All the buses between Bangor and the Isle of Anglesey are funnelled through Menai Bridge, including the no. 4 service from Bangor to Holyhead on weekdays (no. 44 on Sundays).

An excavated medieval house in Newborough Forest

Ynys Llanddwyn

Outline

Newborough Forest car-park – Beach – Ynys Llanddwyn – Beach – Newborough Forest car-park.

Summary

A short visit to the forest to see an old ruin is followed by a long trek over the sands to an island where the Welsh version of St Valentine asked to be able to help lovers.

Attractions

Take a romantic walk to the island for lovers. St Dwynwen was one of King Brychan's 24 daughters (this 5th century ruler of the modern Brecon district also had 12 sons, presumably by several wives). She was very beautiful and fell deeply in love with a handsome young man named Maelon. Her father arranged a dynastic marriage to a prince, however, giving Dwynwen no say in the matter. Maelon was enraged and forced himself upon Dwynwen. Being an obedient girl, she was in an impossible situation. She sought solitude and prayed intensely to God, asking that she be relieved of her great love for Maelon. An angel came in her sleep and administered a potion which cured her of her love. In her dream, she also saw the angel give the same potion to Maelon, turning him to a block of ice.

God then gave Dwynwen three wishes. First she wished that Maelon be thawed, presumably to love again, then she asked that God might answer all requests she made on behalf of lovers and, finally, that she should remain unmarried, becoming a nun. Her wishes were granted and she devoted her life to serving God and lovers. She lived by the maxim 'there is none so lovable as the cheerful'. The 16th century Welsh poet Dafydd Trefor described her as 'the mother of all goodness'. Dwynwen retreated to the island that now bears her name and built a little chapel. She enjoyed a glorious view from her island, whose rocks happen to be some of the oldest in Britain. As she lay dying, Dwynwen asked to be taken to see the sunset one last time. She was carried as far as the shelter of a boulder. It miraculously split apart to grant the saint her dying wish. A cliff-edge boulder is still in place, complete with a 'spy-hole'. Another of the old rocks cured those who slept the night on it of rheumatism. It was known as Gwely Esyth. Ancient rocks have been found to contain certain healing properties.

Lovers soon started to make pilgrimages to St Dwynwen's holy island. The saint had left them a holy well with the power to show if their love was true. An eel lived in the well and if it disturbed a cloth placed over the water then the pilgrim's loved one was unfaithful.

This holy well was still in use this century. It is near the Pilots' Cottages and an eel was still associated with it in the 1950s, when Tom Jones was the resident

Continued on page 74

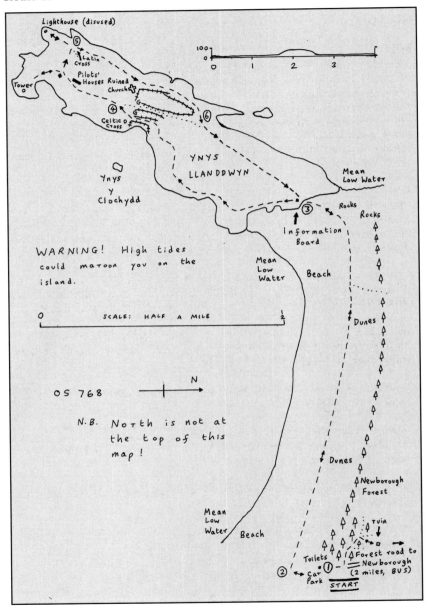

Lighthouse (disused)

⑤

Latin
Cross

Pilots'
Houses   Ruined
Church

Tower

④

Celtic
Cross

⑥

YNYS
LLANDDWYN

Ynys
y
Clochydd

Mean
Low Water

③   Rocks

Rocks

Information
Board

WARNING! High tides
could maroon you on the
island.

Mean
Low
Water   Beach

Dunes

SCALE: HALF   A   MILE

OS 768   N

N.B. North is not at
the top of this
map!

Dunes

Newborough
Forest

Mean
Low
Water   Beach

Twin

Toilets   Forest road to
Newborough
② ← Car   ① (2 miles, BUS)
Park
START

Route 16

Ynys Llanddwyn

4 miles

Start

This walk is described from the car park near the beach in Newborough Forest. This is in the south-west corner of Anglesey. **Add four miles** to the walk if you come by bus. The car-park near the beach in Newborough Forest is at the end of the access lane from Newborough. There is an admission charge for cars. If coming by public transport, alight at the bus stop near the crossroads in Newborough. Face the Spar shop, go right and turn right at the crossroads. Follow the road past St Peter's church on your right and through Newborough Forest to its end, near the beach (GR SH 405634).

Route

1. Take the signposted Forest Walk, to the right of the toilets, for about 400 yards, then turn right at a green-topped post. Follow the track to an old reservoir on your left and come to the ruin of an excavated medieval house ahead. Retrace your steps to the car-park and go right to pass the toilets on your right and reach the beach.

2. Walk along the beach for 1 mile and cross to the island. N.B. THIS MAY BE DANGEROUS AT HIGH SPRING TIDE. DO NOT BE CAUGHT MAROONED ON THE ISLAND NEAR DUSK WITH YOUNG CHILDREN!

3. Take the path waymarked with yellow-topped posts which forks left at the back of an information board. Climb along the cliffs before bearing inland to join the island's central track.

4. Go left along the track to pass the Pilots' Cottages and visit the Tower, then cross to the other side of the island.

5. Visit the old lighthouse, then turn back along a path waymarked with yellow posts that climbs the cliffs and passes the ruins of the church on your right. Bear right to join the central track.

6. Go left along the central track back to the information board. Retrace your steps along the beach back to the car-park.

Public Transport

Newborough is visited by buses nos 42 (from Bangor and Llangefni), 43 (from Bangor) and 45 (from Holyhead and Llangefni) on weekdays.

lighthouse-keeper. It is a source of crystal clear water in a small, deep, rock-bound pool. Writing about her childhood holidays on the island in the 1950s in *Country Quest* (February 1991), Anne Wolf remembered a low corrugated iron hut with a rickety door, recording 'I eagerly sought the eel which Tom kept there to keep the water clean. I rarely saw the fish . . . and when I did, the incident became the highlight of my day'.

Notice the two commemorative crosses. The Celtic one was erected after the discovery of bones nearby in 1903. A Latin cross stands near the other shore and commemorates the saint's death in 465 AD. St Dwynwen's Day is 25th January, so Welsh lovers can exchange cards nearly three weeks earlier than their English counterparts. The commercial side of St Dwynwen's story brought prosperity in the Middle Ages too. The ruined church was built in the 16th century on a grand scale to meet the demand from the large numbers of pilgrims. It is on the site of the saint's original chapel. Her hermitage became an abbey which was destroyed at the Dissolution. The stones were used to build the cottages for the pilots in the early 19th century and for the lighthouse, built in the style of an Anglesey windmill in 1845. An earlier beacon (Twr Bach) had proved ineffective. The pilots guided ships over Caernarfon bar and helped to man the lifeboat station which saved 101 lives between 1853 and 1903. Volunteers from Newborough were alerted by the cannon near the square stone building that housed the lifeboat. Now that the lighthouse is disused, it is ironic that the old tower bears the automatic flashing light. The pilots have gone, along with the need to separate them from their children during the week so that they could attend school in Newborough. One cottage has been refurbished to appear as it was in 1900, another houses an exhibition on the environment and wildlife. Soay sheep graze near the ruins of the church. When the flowers carpet the cliffs in May there could hardly be a more ideal spot.

Newborough Forest has a tale to tell too. The Welsh from Beaumaris were settled here by Edward I. Their houses were covered by windblown sand which has now been stabilised by Corsican pine and Sitka spruce planted since 1947. Medieval ruins have been excavated.

Refreshments
Bring your own picnic and enjoy it on the beach.

Don't get cut off on the island by high spring tides!

The Cannon on Ynys Llanddwyn

Useful information

Approximate mileage of each walk from Menai Bridge, Llangefni and Holyhead via main roads.

Route	Menai Bridge	Llangefni	Holyhead
1	22	18	17
2	17	13	22
3	23	17	1
4	22	16	0
5	19	11	10
6	13	6	18
7	8	14	30
8	18	12	14
9	9	0	16
10	4	13	26
11	16	10	16
12	14	8	18
13	4	6	20
14	2	7	21
15	0	9	22
16	13	10	23

Routes in order of difficulty
None of these routes would be strenuous to an experienced walker. The following grading is made in the context of a Family Walks book and is done with the fairly active 6 or 7 year old in mind.

Easy Walks
Route   3 – Soldier's Point (2¼ miles)
Route   4 – Holyhead Roman Fort (2¼ miles)
Route   8 – Llyn Maelog (2½ miles)
Route 10 – Beaumaris Castle (2½ miles)
Route 13 – Bryn Celli Ddu (2½ miles)
Route 14 – Llanfairpwllgwyngyllgogerychwyrndrobwllllantysiliogogogoch (1½ miles)
Route 15 – Menai Bridge (1¼ miles)

Moderately Difficult
Route   2 – Amlwch (2¼ miles)
Route   5 – Llanddeusant (2¾ miles)
Route   9 – Llangefni (2 miles)
Route 12 – Llyn Coron (2¾ miles)
Route 16 – Ynys Llanddwyn (4 miles)

Strenuous
Route   1 – Cemaes Bay (2½ miles)
Route   6 – Mynydd Bodafon (3 miles)
Route   7 – Penmon Priory (3 miles)
Route   7 – Aberffraw (2 miles)

Public Transport

Never has our public transport system been under so much attack, yet been so needed. Access to the countryside for many people still depends upon maintaining our network of public transport. Even motorists should consider leaving their car at home and travelling by train or bus. Do all we can to support it and the situation will improve! Our children will reap the benefit. The alternative is to see yet more and more cars on more and more roads. The Isle of Anglesey is definitely not a place for that. Its quiet lanes weren't designed for traffic jams. As it is, Gwynedd County Council are doing their best for you to rely on public transport whilst on holiday here. There is a good bus network covering all of the island, plus a useful railway line. The Gwynedd Day Rover ticket offers excellent value at £3.50* per day (£1.75 for children). Use it on any Bws Gwynedd service, The Crosville rover tickets will take you beyond Gwynedd to the furthest flung corners of the Crosville Bus Empire but they are only valid on Crosville buses on the Isle of Anglesey and many buses are run by other companies. Similarly, Crosville produce their own bus timetable but you'll need the excellent Gwynedd County Council public transport map and timetables if you want all of the island's services. Even the trains are shown on this timetable, although you are advised to pick up the British Rail timetable leaflet for the line between Bangor and Holyhead. Many buses run to Bangor, on the mainland. This would allow connections with the Trawscambria coach service from Cardiff and for exploring Anglesey by day trips from Bangor youth hostel. For a free map and timetable, write (enclosing a 9″ × 6″ SAE, 60 g rate stamp) to the County Planning Officer, County Offices, Caernarfon, Gwynedd, LL55 1SH (tel. 0286 679378). Crosville Wales Ltd can be contacted at Beach Road, Bangor, LL57 1AB, Gwynedd, tel. 0248 351879/370295. For details of ferries beweeen Ireland and Holyhead telephone Sealink Stenna (0407 760222) or B & I (0407 762304).

* 1993 prices

The church of St Marcellus and St Marcellinus, Llanddeusant (route 5)

Tourist information addresses
Llanfairpwllgwyngyllgogerychwyrndrobwllllantysiliogogogoch, near the railway station, tel.
0248 713177, open all year. Holyhead, near Salt Island, tel. 0407 762622, open all year.

Wet weather alternatives. Completely or partly under cover. The Isle of Anglesey is fairly
compact and the bus rover ticket so flexible that anywhere on the island could be considered as
an alternative for any particular walk. The following list is far from being comprehensive!

Walk   1: Wylfa Nuclear Power Station.
Walk   2: Amlwch Leisure Centre.
Walk   3: As for route 4.
Walk   4: Holyhead Leisure Centre, Boat Trip to Ireland.
Walk   5: Melin Llynnon.
Walk   6: As for route 9.
Walk   7: As for route 10.
Walk   8: As for route 11.
Walk   9: Plas Arthur Leisure Centre, Oriel Ynys Mon.
Walk 10: Boat Trip to Puffin Island, Beaumaris Castle, Beaumaris Gaol & Court, Canolfan
         Beaumaris, Museum of Childhood.
Walk 11: Coastal Heritage Centre.
Walk 12: Glantraeth Animal Park.
Walk 13: Pili Palas Butterfly Farm, Plas Newydd, Anglesey Sea Zoo.
Walk 14: James Pringle Weavers, Pili Palas Butterfly Farm.
Walk 15: As for routes 10 and 14, plus Caernarfon Castle.
Walk 16: Anglesey Bird World, Anglesey Sea Zoo.

The Priory Church, Penmon (Route 7)

THE FAMILY WALKS SERIES

Family Walks on Anglesey. Laurence Main. ISBN 0 907758 665.

Family Walks in Berkshire & North Hampshire. Kathy Sharp. ISBN 0 907758 371.

Family Walks around Bristol, Bath & the Mendips. Nigel Vile. ISBN 0 907758 193.

Family Walks around Cardiff & the Valleys. Gordon Hindess. ISBN 0 907758 541.

Family Walks in Cheshire. Chris Buckland. ISBN 0 907758 290.

Family Walks in Cornwall. John Caswell. ISBN 0 907758 55X.

Family Walks in the Cotswolds. Gordon Ottewell. ISBN 0 907758 150.

Family Walks on Exmoor & the Quantocks. John Caswell. ISBN 0 907758 460.

Family Walks in South Gloucestershire. Gordon Ottewell. ISBN 0 907758 339.

Family Walks in Gower. Amanda Green. ISBN 0 907758 630.

Family Walks in Hereford and Worcester. Gordon Ottewell. ISBN 0 907758 207.

Family Walks on the Isle of Wight. Laurence Main. ISBN 0 907758 568.

Family Walks in North West Kent. Clive Cutter. ISBN 0 907758 363.

Family Walks in the Lake District. Barry McKay. ISBN 0 907758 401.

Family Walks in Mendip, Avalon & Sedgemoor. Nigel Vile. ISBN 0 907758 41X.

Family Walks in the New Forest. Nigel Vile. ISBN 0 907758 606.

Family Walks in Oxfordshire. Laurence Main. ISBN 0 907758 38X.

Family Walks in the Dark Peak. Norman Taylor. ISBN 0 907758 169.

Family Walks in the White Peak. Norman Taylor. ISBN 0 907758 096.

Family Walks in South Derbyshire. Gordon Ottewell. ISBN 0 907758 614.

Family Walks in South Shropshire. Marian Newton. ISBN 0 907758 304.

Family Walks in Snowdonia. Laurence Main. ISBN 0 907758 320.

Family Walks in the Staffordshire Peaks and Potteries. Les Lumsdon. ISBN 0 907758 347.

Family Walks around Stratford & Banbury. Gordon Ottewell. ISBN 0 907758 495.

Family Walks in Suffolk. C J Francis. ISBN 0 907758 649.

Family Walks around Swansea. Raymond Humphreys. ISBN 0 907758 622.

Family Walks in the Teme Valley. Camilla Harrison. ISBN 0 907758 452.

Family Walks in Three Peaks & Malham. Howard Beck. ISBN 0 907758 428

Family Walks in Mid Wales. Laurence Main. ISBN 0 907758 274.

Family Walks in the North Wales Borderlands. Gordon Emery. ISBN 0 907758 509.

Family Walks in Warwickshire. Geoff Allen. ISBN 0 907758 533.

Family Walks in the Weald of Kent & Sussex. Clive Cutter. ISBN 0 907758 517.

Family Walks in Wiltshire. Nigel Vile. ISBN 0 907758 215.

Family Walks in the Wye Valley. Heather & Jon Hurley. ISBN 0 907758 266.

Family Walks in the North Yorkshire Dales. Howard Beck. ISBN 0 907758 525.

Family Walks in South Yorkshire. Norman Taylor. ISBN 0 907758 258.

Family Walks in West Yorkshire. Howard Beck. ISBN 0 907758 436.

The publishers welcome suggestions for further titles in this series; and will be pleased to consider manuscripts relating to Derbyshire from new or established authors.

Scarthin Books of Cromford, in the Peak District, are also leading second-hand and antiquarian booksellers, and are eager to purchase specialised material, both ancient and modern.

Contact Dr D. J. Mitchell, 0629-823272.